A collection of Graph Programming Interview Questions Solved in C++

Antonio Gulli

"Graph" is the second of a series of 25 Chapters devoted to algorithms, problem solving and C++ programming.

DEDICATION

To my father Elio and my mother Maria.

For your priceless help during all my life

ACKNOWLEDGMENTS

Thanks to Gaetano Mendola for code reviewing

Table of Contents

1. Implementing a direct graph

A graph data structure $G = (V,E)$ involves a finite set of nodes or vertices V and a set of ordered pairs E called edges or arcs connecting two nodes. A graph might have labels associated to the nodes and/or to the edges, thus denoting different attributes (such as names, costs, capacity, length, colours). A direct graph is a graph where the edges are associated to a direction, which is typically represented with an arrow.

A graph   A direct graph

Solution

The first direct graph implementation represents a node and an edge as a C++ struct. In addition a collection of nodes is memorized in a $std::vector$ and all the edges originating from each node are memorized in a $std::forward\_list$. This representation is known as Adjacency list. In this particular implementation each node has a unique identifier NodeID, a label NodeWeight and another label representing the name of the node. Indeed each edge stores the destination NodeID, a label EdgeWeightI representing the weight of the edge and another label representing the name of the edge.

The second direct graph implementation represents a Graph using a matrix of size $(n * n)$ where n is the number of nodes. This representation is known ad Adjacency Matrix.

Code

```
const std::string emptyString;
```

```cpp
//
// Direct Graph
// with Adjacent lists

class Graph
{
public:
        typedef unsigned int NodeID;
        typedef unsigned int EdgeID;
        typedef int NodeWeight;
        typedef int EdgeWeight;

        struct Edge
        {
                Edge(NodeID nid, EdgeWeight wt,
                const std::string & lb)
                : v(nid), w(wt), label(lb)  {};


                const NodeID v;
                const EdgeWeight w;
                const std::string label;
        };

        struct Node
        {
                Node(NodeWeight wt, const std::string & l) :
                        w(wt), label(l){};

                NodeWeight w;
```

```cpp
        std::string label;
};


// all nodes
typedef std::vector<Node> Nodes;
// edges from a node
typedef std::forward_list<Edge> EdgesList;
// all edges (id -> edgeList)
typedef std::vector<EdgesList> Edges;


// allocate |V| lists of edges
Graph(NodeID V = 0, EdgeID E = 0)
{
    if (V)
    {
        _nodes.reserve(V); _outdegree.reserve(V);
    }
    if (E)
        _edges.reserve(E);
};


void reserveNodes(NodeID n)
{ _nodes.reserve(n); _outdegree.reserve(n); }
void reserveEdges(EdgeID n)
{ _edges.reserve(n); }


//
// we can have multiple edge (v1, v2)
void addEdge(NodeID v1,
    NodeID v2,
```

```cpp
            EdgeWeight w = 0,
            const std::string & label = emptyString)
    {
            if (v1 > _nodes.size() || v2 > _nodes.size())
                    return;
            Edge e(v2, w, label);
            _edges[v1].push_front(e);
            _outdegree[v1]++;
    }


    //
    // nodes are unique
    void addNode(NodeWeight w = 0,
            const std::string & label = emptyString)
    {
            EdgesList el;
            Node n(w, label);
            _nodes.push_back(n);    // another node
            _edges.push_back(el);   // with its EdgeList
            _outdegree.push_back(0);
    }


    const EdgesList & edges(NodeID v) const
    { return _edges[v]; };


    Graph::NodeID outdegree(NodeID v) const
    { return _outdegree[v]; }


    const Nodes & nodes() const
    { return _nodes; };
```

```cpp
        NodeID numNodes() const
        { return _nodes.size(); };


        EdgeID numEdges() const
        { return _edges.size(); };

private:
        Edges  _edges;
        Nodes  _nodes;
        std::vector<Graph::NodeID> _outdegree;


        Graph(const Graph& g) = delete;
        Graph& operator=(const Graph& g) = delete;
};


std::ostream & operator << (std::ostream & os,
        const Graph & g)
{
        Graph::NodeID id = 0;
        for (const auto & n : g.nodes())
        {
                os << " node=" << id << " weight=" << n.w <<
                        " label=" << n.label << std::endl;
                for (const auto & e : g.edges(id))
                        os << " ->" << e.v << " w=" << e.w <<
                        " label=" << n.label
                        << " lableEdge=" << e.label << std::endl;
                ++id;
        }
```

```cpp
        return os;
}


//
// Undirect Graph
// with Adjacency Matrix


template<typename T>
class Matrix
{
public:
        Matrix(const Matrix&) = delete;
        Matrix& operator=(const Matrix&) = delete;

        Matrix(unsigned int dim1, unsigned int dim2)
                : _M(new T*[dim1]), _dim1(dim1), _dim2(dim2)
        {
                for (unsigned int i = 0; i < dim1; ++i)
                        _M[i] = new T[dim2];
        }
        Matrix(unsigned int dim1, unsigned int dim2,
                T defaultValue)
                : Matrix(dim1, dim2)
        {
                for (unsigned int i = 0; i < _dim1; ++i)
                for (unsigned int j = 0; j < _dim2; ++j)
                        _M[i][j] = defaultValue;
        }
```

```cpp
Matrix(Matrix&& aMatrix) {

        _dim1 = aMatrix._dim1;

        _dim2 = aMatrix._dim2;

        _M = aMatrix._M;

        aMatrix._dim1 = 0;

        aMatrix._dim2 = 0;

        aMatrix._M = nullptr;

}


~Matrix()
{

        for (unsigned int i = 0; i < _dim1; ++i)

                delete[] _M[i];

        delete[] _M;

}
T & operator()(const unsigned int i,

        const unsigned int j)

{

        return _M[i][j];

}


T & operator()(const unsigned int i,

        const unsigned int j) const

{

        return _M[i][j];

}


unsigned int dim1() const { return _dim1; };

unsigned int dim2() const { return _dim2; };
```

```cpp
        friend std::ostream & operator <<(std::ostream & out,
                const Matrix<T>& m)
        {
                for (unsigned int i = 0; i < m._dim1; ++i){
                        for (unsigned int j = 0; j < m._dim2; ++j)
                                out << m._M[i][j] << ' ';
                        out << std::endl;
                }
                return out;
        }


        void swap(Matrix & other)
        {
                std::swap(_M, other._M);
                std::swap(_dim1, other._dim1);
                std::swap(_dim2, other._dim2);
        }
private:
        T** _M;
        unsigned int _dim1, _dim2;
};
//
// MatrixGraph

class MatrixGraph{
        MatrixGraph& operator=(const MatrixGraph&) = delete;
public:
        typedef unsigned int NodeID;
        typedef int weight;
```

```cpp
MatrixGraph(NodeID numNodes)
      : n(numNodes)

{

      M = new weight*[n];

      for (NodeID i = 0; i < n; ++i)

      {

            M[i] = new weight[n];

            for (NodeID j = 0; j < n; ++j)

                  M[i][j] = 0;

      }

}

~MatrixGraph()

{

      for (NodeID i = 0; i < n; ++i)

            delete[] M[i];

      delete[] M;

}


MatrixGraph(const MatrixGraph& m)

{

      n = m.getNumNodes();

      M = new weight*[n];


      for (NodeID i = 0; i < n; ++i)

      {

            M = new weight*[n];

            memcpy(M[i], m.M[i], sizeof(int)*n);

      }

}
```

```cpp
        NodeID size() const { return n; }


        const weight & operator()(NodeID i, NodeID j) const
                { return M[i][j]; }
        weight & operator()(NodeID i, NodeID j)
                { return M[i][j]; }
        NodeID getNumNodes() const { return n; }


private:
        NodeID n;
        weight **M;
};


std::ostream& operator << (std::ostream & os, const MatrixGraph
& g)
{
        for (MatrixGraph::NodeID i = 0; i < g.size(); ++i){
                for (MatrixGraph::NodeID j = 0;
                        j < g.size(); ++j)
                        os << g(i, j) << ' ';
                os << std::endl;
        }
        return os;
}


void test()
{
        Graph G;
        G.addNode(10, "donald duck");
        G.addNode(1, "daisy duck");
```

```
G.addNode(1, "antonio");
G.addNode(1, "milena");
G.addNode(1, "lorena");
G.addNode(1, "mambo");
G.addNode(1, "salsa");
G.addNode(1, "adriana");

G.addEdge(0, 2);
G.addEdge(1, 2, 10, "important");
G.addEdge(1, 3);
G.addEdge(2, 3);
G.addEdge(2, 5);
G.addEdge(2, 6);
G.addEdge(4, 5);
G.addEdge(5, 5);
G.addEdge(5, 4);
G.addEdge(5, 100);
std::cout << G;

MatrixGraph mgA(5);
    mgA(0, 1) = 3;  mgA(1, 2) = 2; mgA(1, 3) = 2;
    mgA(2, 3) = mgA(3, 4) = 1;  mgA(4, 0) = 1;
    std::cout << mgA;
}
```

2.   Choosing matrices or adjacency lists

Let us assume that we have a direct graph $G = (V, E)$ with n nodes and m edges and that every pointer takes d bits, when is it more appropriate to use a matrix and when is it better to use adjacency lists to represent the graph?

Solution

The matrix needs n^2 bits, while the adjacency lists need n pointers for each starting list of d bits and m cells of $2d$ bits (d for the pointer to the next cell and an additional d for the pointer to the node). Therefore combining all the information, we need to solve in m the formula $n^2 > dn + 2dm$

3. Implementing a BFS visit

Breadth-first-Search (BFS) is a visiting strategy for a graph where a node is first visited and then all adjacent nodes are visited in turn.

Solution

This is a classical interview question which can be implemented by using a simple queue. At the beginning the root node is enqueued and marked as visited. Then a node is dequeued and all the adjacent nodes not yet visited are enqueued for future visit in turn. The process is repeated until the queue is empty.

Code

```cpp
void bfs(const Graph & g, Graph::NodeID nid)
{
        // queue of visited nodes
        std::deque<Graph::NodeID> queue;
        // bfs on unknown node
        if (nid >= g.numNodes())
                return;

        std::vector<bool> visited(g.numNodes(), false);
        visited[nid] = true;
        queue.push_back(nid);
```

```cpp
        std::cout << "Start bfs" << std::endl;


        while (!queue.empty())
        {
                const Graph::NodeID id = queue.front();
                queue.pop_front();
                std::cout << "Visited: " << id << std::endl;


                for (const auto & e : g.edges(id))
                {
                        if (!visited[e.v])
                        {
                                visited[e.v] = true;
                                queue.push_back(e.v);

                        }

                }

        }


        std::cout << "End bfs" << std::endl << std::endl;
}
```

Complexity

Space complexity is $O(|V|)$ for the queue and $O(|V| + |E|)$, if the graph is represented using an adjacency list, or $O(|V|^2)$ if an adjacency matrix is adopted. Time complexity is $(|V| + |E|)$, where $O(|E|)$ may vary between $O(|V|)$ and $O(|V^2|)$, depending on how sparse the graph is.

4.   Erdős number

Solution

Paul Erdős is a famous mathematician who wrote more than 1500 scientific articles. His direct co-authors have distance 1 from him, while their respective co-authors have distance 2. Recursively, whoever has a collaboration with authors at distance $k-1$ from Erdős will therefore be at distance k (also denoted as Erdős (author)=K). The author of this book has Erdős ("Antonio Gulli")=3 because he wrote a paper with "Fabrizio Sebastiani" who, in turn, wrote a paper with "Micheal Anthony Steel", who is a direct co-author of Erdős. Erdős numbers can be computed with a slight variation of the BFS visit and this implementation is left as an exercise.

5.   Implementing a DFS visit

Depth-first-Search (DFS) is a visiting strategy for a graph, where the visit starts from a selected root node and the exploration is run as far as possible along each branch before backtracking to the first not yet visited children.

Solution

This is another classical interview question which can be solved by using either recursion or iteration.

The dfs method implements a recursive solution which starts from the root node sid and it keeps a boolean vector of visited nodes and their colours. For each node the colour is 'w' (white) at the very beginning, 'g' (gray) when the node is visitedand 'b' (black) when all the adjacent nodes are also visited. In addition the time, when the node is visited, is stored in the vector timing.

The dfsStack method implements an iterative solution where the root node is inserted in the stack. Then the top of the stack is removed and all the adjacent not yet visited nodes are put on the stack itself. The process is repeated until the stack is empty.

Code

```cpp
void dfsUtilRich(const Graph & g, Graph::NodeID sid,
        std::vector<bool> & visited,
        std::vector<Graph::NodeID> & colour,
        std::vector<Graph::NodeID> & timing,
        unsigned int & time)
{
        std::cout << "Starting dfsUtilRich on " <<
                sid << std::endl;

        visited[sid] = true;
        colour[sid] = 'g'; // gray
        ++time;
        timing[sid] = time;

        for (const auto & e : g.edges(sid))
        if (!visited[e.v])
                dfsUtilRich(g, e.v, visited, colour, timing,
time);

        colour[sid] = 'b'; //black
        ++time;
}
void dfs(const Graph & g, Graph::NodeID sid)
{
```

```cpp
        if (sid >= g.numNodes())                    // dfs on
unknown node
                return;

        unsigned int time = 0;
        std::vector<bool> visited(g.numNodes(), false);
        // white
        std::vector<Graph::NodeID> colour(g.numNodes(), 'w');
        std::vector<Graph::NodeID> timing(g.numNodes(), 0);

        visited[sid] = true;
        std::cout << "Starting dfs on " <<
                sid << std::endl;

        for (const auto & e : g.edges(sid))
        {
                if (!visited[e.v])
                {
                        visited[e.v] = true;
                        dfsUtilRich(g, e.v, visited,
                                colour, timing, time);
                }
        }
        std::cout << "End dfs" << std::endl << std::endl;
}

void dfsStack(const Graph & g, Graph::NodeID sid)
{
        if (sid >= g.numNodes())        // dfs on unknown node
                return;
```

```cpp
        std::stack<Graph::NodeID> nodesToBeVisited;
        std::vector<bool> visited(g.numNodes(), false);

        visited[sid] = true;
        nodesToBeVisited.push(sid);
        std::cout << "Starting dfs on " << sid << std::endl;

        while (!nodesToBeVisited.empty())
        {
                const Graph::NodeID nid = nodesToBeVisited.top();
                bool myFullExploredNode = true;
                for (const auto & e : g.edges(nid))
                {
                        if (!visited[e.v])
                        {
                                visited[e.v] = true;
                                nodesToBeVisited.push(e.v);
                                std::cout << "Visited: " << e.v <<
std::endl;
                                myFullExploredNode = false;
                                break;
                        3}
                }
                if (myFullExploredNode)
                        nodesToBeVisited.pop();
        }
        std::cout << "End dfs" << std::endl << std::endl;
}
```

Complexity

Space complexity is $O(|V|)$ for the stack and $O(|V| + |E|)$, if the graph is represented using an adjacency list or $O(|V|^2)$ if an adjacency matrix is adopted. Time complexity is $O(|V| + |E|)$, where $O(|E|)$ may vary between $O(|V|)$ and $(|V^2|)$, depending on how sparse the graph is.

6. How to detect a cycle in a graph

Solution

A DFS visit can detect a cycle, if there is a back edge during the visit of the graph. By using the notation defined in the above solution, this condition is represented by a transition from a grey node to a grey node.

Code

This implementation is left as an exercise.

Complexity

The complexity here is the same as DFS.

7. Given two nodes in an undirected graph, find the path connecting them

Solution

A simple solution is to visit the graph with DFS order starting from one of the two nodes and stopping the visit as soon as the other node is found. During this process the visited nodes are stored into a stack. At the end the stack will contain the desired path.

Code

This implementation is left as an exercise.

Complexity

The complexity is the same as DFS.

8. Solving mazes

Let us suppose to have a maze as the one represented in this figure. What is the best way to find the exit?

Solution

The interested reader can think about how to represent the maze with a graph G and what the most appropriate visiting strategies on G are.

9. Given a direct acyclic graph, implement a topological sort

A topological sort of a directed graph is a linear ordering of its vertices such that for every directed edge (u, v) from vertex u to vertex v, u comes before v in the ordering. A topological ordering is possible, if and only if the graph has no directed cycles. Such graphs are called "directed acyclic graphs" (DAG).

Solution

Given a DAG, the topological sort is obtained by visiting the nodes with a BFS and storing the nodes into a stack stk. At the end of the process the stack will contain the topologically sorted nodes. The interested reader should modify the code in order to verify the presence of cycles, if the graph is not a DAG (left as exercise).

Code

```
void topologicalSortUtil(const Graph & g,
        Graph::NodeID sid,
        std::vector<bool> & visited,
        std::stack<Graph::NodeID> &stk)
{
        visited[sid] = true;
        std::cout << "\t topologicalSortUtil"
                << sid << std::endl;

        for (const auto & e : g.edges(sid))
        if (!visited[e.v])
                topologicalSortUtil(g, e.v, visited, stk);

        stk.push(sid);
}

void topologicalSort(const Graph & g)
{
        std::vector<bool> visited(g.numNodes(), false);
        std::stack<Graph::NodeID> stk;

        for (Graph::NodeID nid = 0; nid < g.numNodes(); ++nid)
```

```cpp
        if (!visited[nid])
                topologicalSortUtil(g, nid, visited, stk);


        std::cout << "topologicalSort" << std::endl;


        while (!stk.empty())
        {
                std::cout << stk.top() << std::endl;
                stk.pop();
        }
}
```

Complexity

Time complexity is $O(|V| + |E|)$, space complexity is $O(|V| + |E|)$.

10. Detecting a bipartite graph

A bipartite graph is a graph, in which its vertices can be divided into two disjoint sets U and V.

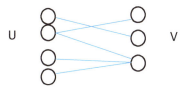

A bipartite graph

Solution

A DFS or a BFS visit can be performed by assigning colors to the graph in such a way that the children have opposite colors from their parents. If two directly connected nodes have same color, the graph is not bipartite.

Code

```cpp
bool isBipartite(const Graph & g, Graph::NodeID sid)
{
        if (sid >= g.numNodes())
                return false;

        std::vector<Graph::NodeID> colour(g.numNodes(), -1);
        colour[sid] = 1;
        std::list<Graph::NodeID> queue;
        queue.push_back(sid);

        while (!queue.empty())
        {
                const Graph::NodeID n = queue.front();
                queue.pop_front();

                std::cout << "Visited=" << n << std::endl;
                for (const auto & e : g.edges(n))
                {
                        if (colour[e.v] == -1)
                        {
                                colour[e.v] = 1 - colour[n];
                                queue.push_back(e.v);
                        }
                        else if (colour[e.v] == colour[n])
                                return false;
                }
        }
        return true;
```

}

Complexity

Time complexity is $O(|V| + |E|)$, space complexity is $O(|V| + |E|)$.

11. Given a connected graph, compute the minimum spanning tree (MST)

Let us start with some definitions. An undirected graph is said to be connected, if every pair of vertices in the graph is connected. In particular, two vertices u and v are defined as connected, if the graph contains a path from u to v. Given a connected graph, a spanning tree is a tree which connects all vertices together. If the graph has weights associated to the edges, then the minimum spanning tree is a spanning tree with minimal sum of the edges' weight.

Solution

One way to compute the MST is to adopt a classical greedy algorithm due to Prim1. At the beginning the tree contains a single vertex, chosen arbitrarily from the graph. Then the minimum weight edge is selected among those connecting a vertex in the tree with a vertex not being in the tree. This edge is added to the tree and the previous step is repeated until all vertices are in the tree. In our implementation the edges are maintained ordered by using a priority queue realized with boost::fibonacci

Code

```
struct nodeComparison
{
    const MatrixGraph::NodeID node;
```

[1] http://en.wikipedia.org/wiki/Prim%27s_algorithm

```cpp
    MatrixGraph::weight priority;

    nodeComparison(MatrixGraph::NodeID name,
        MatrixGraph::NodeID p) : node(name), priority(p) {};

    bool operator < (nodeComparison const & rhs) const
    {
        return priority > rhs.priority;
    }
};
void PrimMST(const MatrixGraph & g, MatrixGraph::NodeID
startNode)
{
    typedef boost::heap::fibonacci_heap< nodeComparison > Heap;

    Heap heap;
    std::map <MatrixGraph::NodeID, Heap::handle_type> mapHandles;
        // for decrease() key

    MatrixGraph::weight edgeWeight;
    MatrixGraph::NodeID numNodes = g.getNumNodes();

    std::vector<bool> isInHeap(numNodes, false);
    std::vector<MatrixGraph::NodeID> parent(numNodes + 1, 0);

    for (MatrixGraph::NodeID i = 0; i < numNodes; ++i)
    {
        mapHandles[i] =
            heap.push(nodeComparison(i,
                std::numeric_limits<MatrixGraph::weight>::max()))
            ;
```

```cpp
    isInHeap[i] = true;
}


(*(mapHandles[startNode])).priority = 0;
      // initial node has priority 0
heap.increase(mapHandles[startNode]);
// fibonacci has increase ammortized constat
// decrease is logaritmic -> inverted operator <


while (!heap.empty()){

  const nodeComparison nc = heap.top(); // extract top
  heap.pop();
  isInHeap[nc.node] = false;      // no longer in heap


  std::cout << "node=" << nc.node << " w="
     << nc.priority << std::endl;


  for (MatrixGraph::NodeID v = 0; v < numNodes; ++v)
  {
    if ((edgeWeight = g(nc.node, v)) // an edge (nc.node, v)
      && (isInHeap[v])                    // v is in Heap
      && (edgeWeight < (*(mapHandles[v])).priority))
          // improving weight
   {
     (*(mapHandles[v])).priority = edgeWeight;
     heap.increase(mapHandles[v]);
     parent[v] = nc.node;
     std::cout << "node=" << nc.node << "->"
            << v << " with w=" <<
```

```
            (*(mapHandles[v])).priority << std::endl;
      }
    }
  }
  std::cout << "MST" << std::endl;
  for (MatrixGraph::NodeID i = 1; i < numNodes; ++i)
  {
    std::cout << parent[i] << '-' << i <<
      " weight=" << g(parent[i], i) << std::endl;
  }
}
```

This particular implementation uses an adjacency matrix and therefore its complexity is $O(V^2)$. However it is possible to get $O(E + V \log V)$ by using adjacent lists and a Fibonacci heap in which a Find-minimum is $O(1)$ amortized time2

adjacency matrix for dense or sparse graph	$O(V^2)$
binary heap and adjacency lists for sparse graph	$O((V + E)\log V) =$ $O(E \log V) = O(V \log V)$
binary heap and adjacency lists for dense graph	$O((V + E) \log V) = O(E \log V) = O(V^2 \log$
Fibonacci heap and adjacency list	$O(E + V \log V)$

2 http://en.wikipedia.org/wiki/Fibonacci_heap

Space complexity evaluation is here left as an exercise. An example of minimum spanning tree is in the picture below

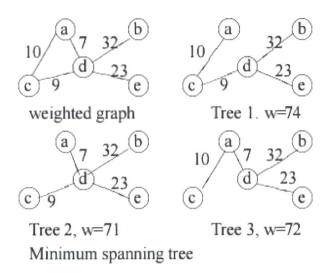

weighted graph

Tree 1. w=74

Tree 2, w=71

Tree 3, w=72

Minimum spanning tree

12. Find the strongly connected components in a direct graph

A direct graph G is said to be strongly connected, if every node is reachable from every other node. The strongly connected components of G create a partition into subgraph that are themselves strongly connected as in this figure.

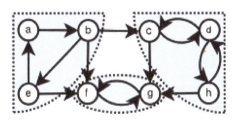

Solution

The here implemented solution is the Kosaraju's algorithm[3] which uses two passes of DFS. The first pass is carried out on the original graph and it is used to choose the order in which the outer loop of the second DFS tests are connected to the vertices. The second DFS is on the transpose graph of the original graph. Each recursive exploration finds a single new strongly connected component.

Code

```
//
// Transpose
void transpose(const Graph & g, Graph & gt)
{
        gt.reserveNodes(g.numNodes());
        gt.reserveEdges(g.numEdges());

        // add all nodes
        for (const auto & n : g.nodes())
                gt.addNode(n.w, n.label);

        // add all edges
        for (Graph::NodeID id = 0; id < g.numNodes(); ++id)
        for (const auto & e : g.edges(id))
                gt.addEdge(e.v, id, e.w, e.label);
}
```

//
———————————————————

[3] http://en.wikipedia.org/wiki/Kosaraju%27s_algorithm

```cpp
// SCC
void fillOrder(const Graph & g, Graph::NodeID v,
        std::vector<bool> & visited,
        std::stack<Graph::NodeID> &stk)
{
        visited[v] = true;

        for (const auto & e : g.edges(v))
        if (!visited[e.v])
                fillOrder(g, e.v, visited, stk);

        stk.push(v);
}


void StrongConnectedComponents(const Graph & g)
{
        std::stack<Graph::NodeID> stk;
        std::vector<bool> visited(g.numNodes(), false);
        unsigned componentID = 0;

        for (Graph::NodeID id = 0; id < g.numNodes(); ++id)
        if (visited[id] == false)
                fillOrder(g, id, visited, stk);

        Graph gt;
        transpose(g, gt);

        std::fill(visited.begin(), visited.end(), false);

        while (!stk.empty())
```

```
{
        Graph::NodeID id = stk.top();
        stk.pop();

        if (!visited[id])
        {
                dfsUtil(g, id, visited);
                std::cout << "end component id="
                        << componentID++ << std::endl;
        }
    }
}
```

Complexity

Time complexity is here $O(V + E)$

13. Covering DFS Trees

Given a graph G it is possible to define a path tree T generated by a DFS visit. If G is not (strongly) connected then we need to restart the DFS from each node and the visit will generate a forest of trees, If the graph is direc,t the visit will respect the direction of the edges, while if the graph is not direct, the visit will produce a random orientation of each edge as a consequence of the direction of the visit. During the visit the edges not yet included in T can be divided into three categories:

- If the edge is examined by passing from a node u in T to another node v in T, which is an ancestor of u in G, then the edge (u, v) is called loop back edge
- If the edge is examined by passing from a node u in T to another node v in T, which is a descendant of u in G, then the edge (u, v) is called forward edge

- Otherwise it is called cross edge

14. Find an Hamiltonian cycle

A Hamiltonian path is a path through a graph that visits each node exactly once. If the path is also a cycle, then we have a Hamiltonian cycle as in the figure. The problem is NP-Complete so the worst case solution needs exponential time in the number of nodes.

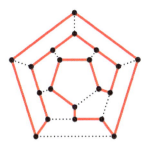

Solution

Here we present a backtracking algorithm in C++

Code

```
// hamiltonianCycle


bool isSafe(const MatrixGraph& g,
        const MatrixGraph::NodeID v,
        std::vector<MatrixGraph::NodeID> & path,
        const unsigned int pos)
{
        if (!g(path[pos - 1], v))
                return false;

        for (MatrixGraph::NodeID i = 0; i < pos; ++i)
        if (path[i] == v)
```

```cpp
            return false;

        return true;
    }


    bool hamiltonianCycleUtil(const MatrixGraph & g,
            std::vector<MatrixGraph::NodeID> & path,
            const unsigned int pos)
    {
        if (pos == g.getNumNodes())
        {
            if (g(path[pos - 1], path[0]))
                    return true;
            else
                    return false;
        }


        for (MatrixGraph::NodeID v = 1; v < g.getNumNodes();
        ++v)
        {
            if (isSafe(g, v, path, pos))
            {
                    path[pos] = v;    // insert v

                    if (hamiltonianCycleUtil(g, path,
                        pos + 1) == true)
                        return true;

                    path[pos] = -1;   // remove v
            }
```

```cpp
        }

    return false;

}


bool hamiltonianCycle(const MatrixGraph & g)
{
    MatrixGraph::NodeID V = g.getNumNodes();
    std::vector<MatrixGraph::NodeID>path(V, -1);
    bool returnValue;

    path[0] = 0;
    if ((returnValue = hamiltonianCycleUtil(g, path, 1)))
    {
        std::cout << "Hamiltionian cycle " << std::endl;
        for (MatrixGraph::NodeID i = 0; i < V; ++i)
            std::cout << path[i] << ' ';
        std::cout << std::endl;

    }
    else {
        std::cout << "No Hamiltionian cycle";
    }
    return returnValue;

}
```

15. Find the articulation points in a graph

An articulation point is any vertex, where its removal increases the number of connected components.

Solution

The algorithm proposed is due to Hopcroft and Tarjan[4]. The idea is to run a DFS while maintaining:

the depth of each vertex in the DFS tree

- For each node v, the lowest depth of neighbours of all descendants of v in the DFS tree, called the lowpoint. The lowpoint of v can be computed after visiting all descendants of v as the minimum of the depth of v, the depth of all neighbors of v (excluding the parent of v in the DFS tree) and the lowpoint of all children of v in the DFS tree.

- A non-root vertex v is an articulation point, if and only if there is a child y of v such that $lowpoint(y) \geq depth(v)$. This property can be tested, once the depth-first search is returned from every child of v. The root vertex must be handled separately: it is an articulation point, if and only if it has at least two children.

Code

```
//
// Articulation Points

void articulationUtil(const Graph & g,
        const Graph::NodeID u,
        unsigned int & time,
```

_____

[4] http://en.wikipedia.org/wiki/Biconnected_component

```cpp
    std::vector<bool> & visited,
    std::vector<Graph::NodeID> & discovery,
    std::vector<Graph::NodeID> & lower,
    std::vector<Graph::NodeID> & parent,
    std::vector<bool> & articulationPoints)
{

    Graph::NodeID children = 0;
    visited[u] = true;
    discovery[u] = lower[u] = ++time;

    for (const auto & e : g.edges(u))
    {
        if (!visited[e.v])
        {
            parent[e.v] = u;
            children++;
            articulationUtil(g, e.v, time, visited,
                    discovery, lower, parent,
                    articulationPoints);

            lower[u] = std::min(lower[u], lower[e.v]);

            if (parent[u] ==

std::numeric_limits<Graph::NodeID>::max()
                    && children > 1)
                articulationPoints[u] = true;

            if (parent[u] ==
```

```cpp
            std::numeric_limits<Graph::NodeID>::max()
                            && lower[e.v] >= discovery[u])
                    articulationPoints[u] = true;
        }
        else if (e.v != parent[u])
                lower[u] = std::min(lower[u],
                    discovery[e.v]);
    }
}


void articulationPoints(const Graph & g)
{
    unsigned int time = 0;
    std::vector<bool> visited(g.numNodes(), false);
    std::vector<Graph::NodeID> discovery(g.numNodes(), 0);
    std::vector<Graph::NodeID> lower(g.numNodes(), 0);
    std::vector<Graph::NodeID> parent(g.numNodes(),
        std::numeric_limits<Graph::NodeID>::max());
    std::vector<bool> articulationPoints(g.numNodes(),
        false);

    for (Graph::NodeID id = 0; id < g.numNodes(); ++id)
    if (!visited[id])
            articulationUtil(g, id, time, visited, discovery,
                lower, parent, articulationPoints);

    for (Graph::NodeID id = 0; id < g.numNodes(); ++id)
    if (articulationPoints[id])
            std::cout << "articulation point id=" <<
```

```
        id << std::endl;
}
```

Complexity

Time complexity is $O(V + E)$. An example of articulation point is in the picture below

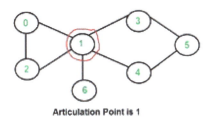

Articulation Point is 1

16. Find the shortest path in a graph with non-negative edge weight

Solution

Given a graph with non-negative edge weight, we can apply Dijkstra's algorithm for finding the single-source shortest path tree. Edger Dijkstra was born in the Netherlands and he invented the algorithm in 1959. For a given source node s, the algorithm looks for the path with lowest cost between s and every other node. This class of problems has multiple applications including optimization, routing and traffic assignment. The pseudo-code for Dijkstra is given below. The vector $d[u]$ contains the sum of weights for the path used to arrive to the node u (at the beginning this is infinite). The vector $p[u]$ contains the predecessor of u in the shortest path (at the beginning $p[u] = u$). In addition a priority queue Q is used to select nodes u with the smallest $dist[n]$ (in the pseudo-code this is the operation u ← EXTRACT-MIN(Q))). Moreover, $Adj[u]$contains all the nodes v adjacent to u. So for each $\in Adj[u]$, if $d[u]$ - the sum of weights for the path leading to u - plus to the weight of the edge $w(u, v)$ is less than $d[v]$ - the sum of the weights for the path leading to v - then we have identified a shorter path. In this case, $d[v]$ and $p[v]$ are updated accordingly. Also the node v is added to Q, if it has never been visited before. Instead, if it has been already visited, its priority in Q should be reduced according to the new weight (this is the operation DECREASE-KEY(Q, v) in the pseudo-code). At the end the vectors d and p are returned.

Code

```
DIJKSTRA(G, s, w)
  for each vertex u in V
     d[u] ← infinity
     p[u] ← u
     color[u] ← WHITE

     color[s] ← GRAY
     d[s] ← 0
     INSERT(Q, s)
     while (Q != ∅)
        u ← EXTRACT-MIN(Q)
        for each vertex v in Adj[u]
           if (w(u,v) + d[u] < d[v])
              d[v] ← w(u,v) + d[u]
              p[v] ← u
              if (color[v] ==  WHITE)
                 color[v] ←  GRAY
                 INSERT(Q,  v)
              else if (color[v] == GRAY)
```

DECREASE-KEY(Q, v)

color[u] ← BLACK

return (d, p)

For this exercise we start using boost::BGL a powerful framework for graph creation and processing[5]. A graph can have weights and names labels associated to the edges and those are stored in a boost::property. In addition a graph can be represented either with a boost::adjacency_list or with a boost:adjacenty_matrix. The boost:adjacenty_list uses many parameters including OutEdgeList (the selector for the container used to represent the edge-list for each of the vertices), VertexList (the selector for the container used to represent the vertex-list of the graph), Directed (a selector to choose whether the graph is directed, undirected, or directed with bidirectional edge access), VertexProperties (for specifying internal property storage), EdgeProperties (for specifying internal property storage), GraphProperties (for specifying property storage for the graph object) , EdgeList (the selector for the container used to represent the edge-list for the graph). For instance, listS selects std::list and this is a good choice, if you need to add and remove vertices quickly. The adjacency_list class implements boost::property_maps for accessing objects (properties) that are attached to the vertices and edges of the graph, and boost::iterator_property_map is used to navigate inside the maps. All these features are used to represent multiple flavours of graphs with an uniform representation. Having this contest in mind, we can create a Graph g and add vertices and edges with the appropriate boost method. The predecessorMap records the edges in the shortest path tree, the tree is computed by the graph traversal,

---

[5] http://www.boost.org/doc/libs/1_55_0/libs/graph/doc/index.html

while the shortest path weight from the source vertex to each vertex in the graph g is recorded in the distanceMap. In this particular example we compute the shortest path starting from a specific source node v3 and we extract the shortest path by following the computed precedessorMap

```cpp
#include <boost/graph/adjacency_list.hpp>

#include <boost/graph/dijkstra_shortest_paths.hpp>

#include <boost/graph/graph_traits.hpp>

#include <boost/graph/iteration_macros.hpp>

#include <boost/graph/properties.hpp>

#include <boost/property_map/property_map.hpp>


void boostDijkstra()
{
        typedef float Weight;


        //
http://www.boost.org/doc/libs/1_55_0/libs/graph/doc/property.html
        typedef boost::property<boost::edge_weight_t,
                Weight> WeightProperty;
        typedef boost::property<boost::vertex_name_t,
                std::string> NameProperty;


        //
http://www.boost.org/doc/libs/1_53_0/libs/graph/doc/adjacency_list.html
        typedef boost::adjacency_list < boost::listS,
                boost::vecS, boost::directedS,
                NameProperty, WeightProperty > Graph;
```

```cpp
        // 
http://www.boost.org/doc/libs/1_55_0/libs/graph/doc/graph_trait
s.html
        typedef boost::graph_traits < Graph >::vertex_descriptor
Node;


        typedef boost::property_map < Graph,
                boost::vertex_index_t >::type IndexMap;
        typedef boost::property_map < Graph,
                boost::vertex_name_t >::type NameMap;


        // 
http://www.boost.org/doc/libs/1_37_0/libs/property_map/iterator
_property_map.html
        typedef boost::iterator_property_map < Node*, IndexMap,
                Node, Node& > PredecessorMap;
        typedef boost::iterator_property_map < Weight*,
IndexMap,
                Weight, Weight& > DistanceMap;


        Graph g;


        Node v0 = boost::add_vertex(std::string("v0"), g);
        Node v1 = boost::add_vertex(std::string("v1"), g);
        Node v2 = boost::add_vertex(std::string("v2"), g);
        Node v3 = boost::add_vertex(std::string("v3"), g);


        boost::add_edge(v0, v1, 15, g);
        boost::add_edge(v1, v3, 7, g);
        boost::add_edge(v0, v2, 2, g);
        boost::add_edge(v2, v3, 4, g);
```

```cpp
std::vector<Node> predecessors(boost::num_vertices(g));
std::vector<Weight> distances(boost::num_vertices(g));


IndexMap indexMap = boost::get(boost::vertex_index, g);
PredecessorMap predecessorMap(&predecessors[0],
        indexMap);
DistanceMap distanceMap(&distances[0], indexMap);


boost::dijkstra_shortest_paths(g, v0,

boost::distance_map(distanceMap).predecessor_map(predece
ssorMap));


std::cout << "distances and parents:" << std::endl;
NameMap nameMap = boost::get(boost::vertex_name, g);


BGL_FORALL_VERTICES(v, g, Graph)
{
        std::cout << "distance(" << nameMap[v0] << ", "
                << nameMap[v] << ") = " << distanceMap[v]
                << ", ";
        std::cout << "predecessor(" << nameMap[v]
                << ") = "
                << nameMap[predecessorMap[v]] << std::endl;
}
std::cout << std::endl;


typedef std::vector<Graph::edge_descriptor> PathType;
```

```cpp
PathType path;

Node v = v3;
for (Node u = predecessorMap[v];
        u != v;
        v = u, u = predecessorMap[v])
{
        std::pair<Graph::edge_descriptor, bool> edgePair
                boost::edge(u, v, g);
        Graph::edge_descriptor edge = edgePair.first;

        path.push_back(edge);
}

float totalDistance = 0;
for (PathType::reverse_iterator pathIterator =
        path.rbegin();
        pathIterator != path.rend(); ++pathIterator)
{
        std::cout <<
                nameMap[boost::source(*pathIterator, g)]
                << " -> " <<
                nameMap[boost::target(*pathIterator, g)]
                << " = " <<
                boost::get(boost::edge_weight, g,
                *pathIterator)
        << std::endl;
}
```

```
std::cout << "Distance: "
    << distanceMap[v2] << std::endl;
}
```

A useful exercise is to use Dijkstra for computing the shortest path on the graph represented in picture.

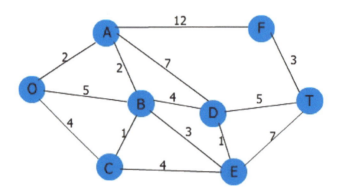

Complexity

Time complexity is $O(|V|log|V| + |E|)$, if the priority queue is implemented using Fibonacci heaps. Fibonacci heap is a priority queue which implements extracting minimum efficiently. Note that Dijkstra's original algorithm does not use a min-priority queue and runs in time $O(|V^2|)$.

17. Find MST(Minimum Spanning Tree) using Kruskal Algorithm

Kruskal's algorithm finds a minimum spanning tree (MST) in an undirected graph with weighted edges. The algorithm orders the edges for increasing weight and then every single edge is included in the solution, if it does not form a cycle with the edges already selected.

Solution

The pseudo code uses UNION-FIND operations[6]:

- Find: Determine which subset a particular element is in. It is used for determining, if two elements are in the same subset.
- Union: Join two subsets into a single subset.

```
KRUSKAL-MST(G, w)
   T ← ∅
   for each vertex u in V
     MAKE-SET(DS, u)


   for each edge (u,v) in E in order of nondecreasing
weight
      if FIND-SET(DS, u) != FIND-SET(DS, v)
        UNION-SET(DS, u, v)
        T ← T U {(u,v)}


  return T
```

[6] http://en.wikipedia.org/wiki/Disjoint-set_data_structure

In boost, this is defined in
boost/graph/kruskal_min_spanning_tree.hpp

As an exercise try to compute Kruskal on the following graph

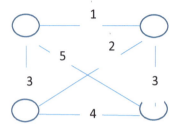

Complexity

Time complexity is $O(E \log E)$ because we use union-find data structure to keep the set information, where Find operations on n elements require $O(n \log n)$ time.

18. Find the longest path in a DAG

The problem of finding the longest path is NP-hard for a general graph. However if we have a DAG, we can easily compute the topological sort. Then for every node we update the distance of its adjacent nodes by using the distance of current vertex.

Solution

This code uses the topological sort defined before and then adds weights starting from the source

Code

```
void longestPathDAG(const Graph & g,
        const Graph::NodeID id,
        std::vector<Graph::NodeID>& distance)
```

```cpp
{
    std::stack<Graph::NodeID> stk;
    distance = std::vector<Graph::NodeID>(g.numNodes(),
        std::numeric_limits<Graph::NodeID>::max());
    std::vector<bool> visited(g.numNodes(), false);

    distance[id] = 0;

    for (Graph::NodeID id = 0; id < g.numNodes(); ++id)
    if (!visited[id])
        topologicalSortUtil(g, id, visited, stk);

    while (!stk.empty())
    {
        const Graph::NodeID id = stk.top();
        stk.pop();

        if (distance[id] !=
            std::numeric_limits<Graph::NodeID>::max())
        {
            for (const auto & e : g.edges(id))
            if (distance[e.v] > distance[id] + e.w)
                distance[e.v] = distance[id] + e.w;
        }
    }
    for (Graph::NodeID id = 0; id < g.numNodes(); ++id)
    if (distance[id] ==
      std::numeric_limits<Graph::NodeID>::max())
        std::cout << "id=" << id <<
        " has infinity distance" << std::endl;
```

```
    else
            std::cout << "id=" << id <<
            " has distance=" << distance[id] << std::endl;
}
```

Complexity

Time complexity is $O(V + E)$. What is the space complexity?

19. Find MST (Minimum Spanning Tree) using Prim Algorithm

Prim's algorithm finds a minimum spanning tree (MST) in an undirected graph with weighted edges. Prim's is a typical greedy algorithm which maintains two data structures $p[v]$ containing the predecessor of the node v and $d[v]$, containing the minimum distance from node v. At the beginning every node is marked as not visited and the distance is infinite. Then the source node s is inserted in a priority queue Q ordered by distance d. Until the queue is not empty a node u is de-queued from Q. For each node v adjacent to u the condition $w(u,v) < d[v]$ is checked where $w(u,v)$ is the weight associated to the edge (u,v). The node v is inserted in Q, if the condition is met and the node was never visited before. Instead if priority is decreased, the condition is met but the node is already in Q.

Solution

The pseudo code is the following:

```
PRIM-MST(G, s, w)
  for each vertex u in V[G]
     color[u] ←  WHITE; d[u] ←  infinity

     color[s] ←  GRAY; d[s] ←  0
```

```
ENQUEUE(Q, s); p[s] ← s
while (Q != Ø)
  u := DEQUEUE(Q)
  for each v in Adj[u]
    if (w(u,v) < d[v])
      d[v] ← w(u,v); p[v] ← u
      if (color[v] = WHITE)
        ENQUEUE(Q, v) ;color[v] ← GRAY
      else if (color[v] = GRAY)
        DECREASE-KEY(Q, v)


  color[u] ← BLACK


return (p, d)
```

In boost, this is defined in
boost/graph/prim_minimum_spanning_tree.hpp

Complexity

Time complexity is $O(V log V + E log V)$ where $V log V$ is the time needed for extracting V nodes from Q and $E log V$ is the time needed for processing the adjacency list and update the queue. Note that if we use Fibonacci heap, then operations of insert and decreaseKey have cost $O(1)$ amortized by deleteKey with cost $O(log V)$. So complexity is $O(V log V + E)$ by using Fibonacci

20. Find all pairs shortest paths using the Floyd-Warshall Algorithm

Floyd & Warshall's algorithm finds the shortest distance between every pair of vertices in the graph. The algorithm detects, if there are loops with negative weights, which will produce a degenerate negative infinite shortest path otherwise.

Solution

The pseudo-code is

```
let dist be a |V| × |V| array of min distances
initialized to ∞
   for each vertex v
      dist[v][v] ← 0
   for each edge (u,v)
      dist[u][v] ← w(u,v)   // the weight for edge (u, v)
   for k from 1 to |V|
      for i from 1 to |V|
         for j from 1 to |V|
            if dist[i][j] > dist[i][k] + dist[k][j]
               dist[i][j] ← dist[i][k] + dist[k][j]
```

This pseudo-code computes the weight of each shortest path between all pair of nodes (i, j) in the graph. However, it does not memorize the minimum paths. These can be stored with some changes in the code which are here left for exercise.

Now let's consider a negative cycle which is a cycle whose edges sum to a negative value. There is no shortest path between any pair of nodes (i, j) which form a part of a negative cycle, because path-lengths from i to j can be arbitrarily small. As an exercise we ask to modify the pseudo-code for detecting negative cycles.

In boost this is defined in

boost/graph/floyd_warshall_shortest.hpp

Complexity

Time complexity is $O(V^3)$, while space complexity is $O(V^2)$

21. Find all the single source shortest paths using Bellman Ford Algorithm

The Bellman-Ford algorithm finds the single-source shortest paths problem for a graph with both positive and negative edge weights. Dijkstra's algorithm is more efficient for a graph with only positive edge weights. Bellman Ford is the code of the old RIP7 (Routing Internet Protocol). Bellman-Ford is very similar to Dijkstra but it processes all the edges instead of selecting the node with minimum weight among those that still have to be processed (greedy choice). This computation is repeated for all the nodes.

Solution

The pseudo-code is the following:

```
BELLMAN-FORD(G)
  for each vertex u in V
    d[u] ← infinity; p[u] ← u

  for i ← 1 to |V|-1
    for each edge (u,v) in E
        if (w(u,v) + d[u] < d[v])
                d[v] ← w(u,v) + d[u];
                p[v] ← u

  for each edge (u,v) in E
```

---

[7] http://en.wikipedia.org/wiki/Routing_Information_Protocol

```
if (w(u,v) + d[u] < d[v])
    return (false, , )


return (true, p, d)
```

In boost this is defined in
boost/graph/bellman_ford_shortest_paths.hpp

Complexity

Time complexity is $O(|V||E|)$

22.Independent set of intervals

Given a set of n intervals in the real line, a maximum independent set is a subset X of intervals with maximum size such that any pair of intervals in X has empty intersection.

Solution

Without losing in generality, let us assume that the intervals $[a_1, b_1]....[a_n, b_n]$ have 2 distinct bounds. Let us add to additional intervals $[a_0, b_0]$ and $[a_{n+1}, b_{n+1}]$ such that $b_0 < a_u$ and $a_u < a_{n+1}$ for $1 \le u \le n$. We can build an acyclic graph G with $n+2$ nodes corresponding to the $n+2$ intervals such that there is an edge (u,v), if and only if $b_u < a_v$. Then we assign the weight $w(u, v) = \begin{cases} 0 & u = 0 \\ 1 & othewise \end{cases}$ to each edge (u,v). It can be verified that the shortest path on G defines the independent set of intervals.

Complexity

G is a DAG and can be built in $O(n^2)$ and therefore the shortest path can be computed in $O(n^2)$.

23. Dominant set of intervals

Given a set of n intervals in the real line, a dominant set is a subset X of intervals with minimum size, such that any interval which is not in X has non-empty intersection with the intervals in X.

Solution

Let us make the same assumptions of the previous exercise: we will construct a new graph G. For each interval $[a_u, b_u]$ with $u = 0, 1, ...n$ define $P_u = \{k:a_u < a_k < b_u < b_k\}$ and $Q_u = \{k:a_k > b_u \text{ and } \nexists$ h: $b_u < a_h < b_h < a_k\}$ and introduce and edge (u, v). if and only if $\in P_u \cup Q_u$. Then we assign the weight $w(u, v) = \begin{cases} 0 & u = 0 \\ 1 & othewise \end{cases}$. It can be verified that the shortest path on G defines a dominant set of intervals.

Complexity

G is a DAG and can be built in $O(n^2)$ and therefore the shortest path can be computed in $O(n^2)$.

24. Weighted dominant set of intervals

Given a set of n intervals in the real line where each interval has an associated weight integer and a non-negative. Find a dominant set with minimum weight.

Solution

Left as an exercise

25. Weighted shortest paths with cost associated to the nodes

Suppose that the cost is associated to the nodes instead that to the edges and that therefore the cost of a path is the sum of all the nodes it contains. According to this assumption compute the all pair shortest path.

Solution

A solution can be easily computed associating to each (u, v) the new weight $w1(u, v) = w(u)$. However, all the paths should increase the weight by a constant w(root), because the root is not crossed by any edge

26. Find the flow network using Ford–Fulkerson'Algorithm

A flow network (also known as a transportation network) is a directed graph, where each edge (u,v) has a capacity $C(u,v)$ and receives a flow $f(u,v)$ that cannot exceed $C(u,v)$. The amount of flow into a node must be equal to the amount of flow out of it. However, a source has a more outgoing flow and a sink has a more incoming flow. A network can be used to model traffic information, currents in an electrical circuit and similar problems.

Solution

The pseudo-code is the following:
Given a Network $G = (V, E)$ with flow capacity C, a source node s, and a sink node t, compute a flow f from s to t of maximum value

1. $f(u,v) \leftarrow 0$ for all edges (u, v)
2. While there is a path P from s to t in Gf, such that $C_f(u, v) > 0$ for all edges (u, v) :

1. Find $C_f(p) = \min\{C_f(u, v):(u,v) \in P)$
2. For each edge $(u,v) \in P)$
    1. $f(u,v) \leftarrow f(u,v) + C_f(p)$
    2. $f(v,u) \leftarrow f(v,u) - C_f(p)$

where $G_f(V, E_f)$ is the residual graph when f flow is sent over the network where the capacity $c_f(u, v) = c(u, v) - f(u,v)$ and there is no flow.

The algorithm is defined in

`boost/graph/edmonds_karp_max_flow.hpp`

Complexity

It can be proven that Ford-Fulkerson has time complexity is $O(Ef)$ where f is the maximum flow in the graph. A variant of Ford-Fulkerson known as Edmon-Karp has proven complexity $O(V E^2)$

27. Assignment matching problem

The assignment matching problem consists in finding a maximum weight matching for a given weighted bipartite graph.

Assume that we have n workers and n tasks to be completed. For each pair (worker, task) we know the costs that should be paid per worker to conclude the task. The goal is to conclude all the tasks and to minimize the total cost, under the condition that each worker can execute only one task and vice versa.

Solution

Let $C(i,j)$ the cost matrix for the worker i to conclude the task j and let $A(i,j)$ the assignment matrix when the worker i has assigned the task j. Clearly,
$$\sum_{j=1}^{n} A(i,j) = 1 \quad \text{and} \quad \sum_{i=1}^{n} A(i,j) = 1$$
and we want to minimize the total cost function
$$\sum_{j=1}^{n}\sum_{i=1}^{n} C(i,j)A(i,j)$$
. Note that the costs-matrix can be represented as a complete bipartite graph as in the following example:

6	9	3
4	8	2
2	5	3

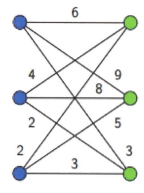

Given this representation, the problem can be solved as a special instance of min cost flow and the solution is left as an exercise.

28. Find an Eulerian circuit

An Eulerian path is a visit in a graph which touches every edge exactly once. If such a walk exists, the graph is said semi-eulerian or traversable. An Eulerian circuit is an Eulerian visit which starts and ends on the same vertex. These problems were first discussed by Leonhard Euler for solving the famous problem of Seven Bridges of Konigsberg[8].

The city of Königsberg in Prussia was built on both sides of the Pregel river, and had two large islands which were connected to each other and the mainland by seven bridges The problem was to find a walk through the city that would cross each bridge once and only once. Euler proved that the problem has no solution and this problem is considering the first one introducing a new discipline called graph theory, the subject of this book.

Solution

At first glance the problem seems similar to the Hamiltonian path. However it is not. Indeed a solution can be computed in linear time.

We notice that a graph has Eulerian cycle if: (a) All vertices with non-zero degree are connected b) All vertices have even degree. In addition, a graph follows the Eulerian Path, if following two conditions hold: (a) All vertices with non-zero degree are connected, (b) If zero or two vertices have odd degree and all other vertices have even degree. The proof of these properties is left as an exercise.

Code

```
bool isConnected(const Graph & g)
{
        std::vector<bool> visited(g.numNodes(), false);
        std::vector<Graph::NodeID> color(g.numNodes(), false);
        std::vector<Graph::NodeID> timing(g.numNodes(), 0);
```

```cpp
        Graph::NodeID id;

        for (id = 0; id < g.numNodes(); ++id)
        if (g.outdegree(id))
                break;

        if (id == g.numNodes())
                return true;

        dfsUtil(g, id, visited);

        for (id = 0; id < g.numNodes(); ++id)
        if (visited[id] == false && g.outdegree(id))
                return false;

        return true;
}


enum euler { notEulerian, SemiEulerian, Eulerian };


//
// Eulerian

euler isEulerian(const Graph & g)
{
        if (isConnected(g) == false)
                return notEulerian;

        unsigned int odd = 0;
        for (Graph::NodeID id = 0; id < g.numNodes(); ++id)
```

```
    if (g.outdegree(id) & 1)
            odd++;


    if (odd > 2)
            return notEulerian;


    return (odd) ? SemiEulerian : Eulerian;
}
```

Complexity

Time complexity is $O(V + E)$

29. Program Scheduling

Given n programs $P1, ..., Pn$ which require $T1, ...,Tn$ time for being executed and an acyclic relation of dependency such that $Pi < Pj$, if program Pi must be executed before Pj find an algorithm which minimizes the total execution time and respects the dependency relation

Solution

We can define a DAG $G = (N, E)$ with n nodes and $(i,j) \in E$ if and only if $Pi < Pj$. If we compute the topological sort of G, the sorted sequence of nodes is the solution. Each node can start just after the moment given by the sum of all the preceding nodes in the sorted order

Complexity

Complexity is $O(n + m)$, where $|N| = n$ and $|E| = m$

ABOUT THE AUTHOR

An experienced data mining engineer, passionate about technology and innovation in consumers' space. Interested in search and machine learning on massive dataset with a particular focus on query analysis, suggestions, entities, personalization, freshness and universal ranking. Antonio Gullì has worked in small startups, medium (Ask.com, Tiscali) and large corporations (Microsoft, RELX). His carrier path is about mixing industry with academic experience.

Antonio holds a Master Degree in Computer Science and a Master Degree in Engineering, and a Ph.D. in Computer Science. He founded two startups, one of them was one of the earliest search engine in Europe back in 1998. He filed more than 20 patents in search, machine learning and distributed system. Antonio wrote several books on algorithms and currently he serves as (Senior) Program Committee member in many international conferences. Antonio teaches also computer science and video game programming to hundreds of youngsters on a voluntary basis.

"Nowadays, you must have a great combination of research skills and a just-get-it-done attitude."

www.ingramcontent.com/pod-product-compliance
Lightning Source LLC
Chambersburg PA
CBHW041144050326
40689CB00001B/481